MW01242278

50 Bible Activities for Creative Minds

Reproducible Classroom Activities for Any Bible Lesson

Written by
Jenifer Hosch

Cover Art by Becky Radtke

CONCORDIA PUBLISHING HOUSE · SAINT LOUIS

Published by Concordia Publishing House
3558 S. Jefferson Avenue
St. Louis, MO 63118-3968

Text copyright © 2003 Jenifer Hosch
Illustrations © 2003 Concordia Publishing House

All rights reserved. Unless specifically noted, no part of this publication may be reproduced,
stored in a retrieval system, or transmitted, in any form or by any means, electronic, mechanical,
photocopying, recording, or otherwise, without the prior written permission of Concordia Publishing House.

Teachers who purchase this product may reproduce pages for use in the classroom and to send home
for parents to use with children.

Scripture quotations are taken from the HOLY BIBLE, NEW INTERNATIONAL VERSION®. NIV®. Copyright © 1973, 1978,
1984 by International Bible Society. Used by permission of Zondervan Publishing House. All rights reserved.

Manufactured in the United States of America

1 2 3 4 5 6 7 8 9 10   12 11 10 09 08 07 06 05 04 03

CONTENTS

Dear Bible Teacher,

You have taken on one of the most exciting tasks imaginable. Just think of it—sharing God's Word with young children! Moms and dads asked you to assist them in raising their children. Furthermore, as a Christian teacher you get to help children understand what it means to live out a baptized life. Your own Baptism and love for the Lord help you to help them learn about the Bible and about God's gifts of Baptism and the Lord's Supper.

The curriculum and lesson plans you already use are excellent tools for the job. But from time to time, you may find that additional resources would help you communicate a concept or teach a fact. That's where this book comes in.

The 50 activity starters offered here were developed from my own experience as a Bible teacher. I think of these pages as springboards to great projects. Each activity is designed to be a starting point, not a worksheet but a *working* sheet.

The projects are somewhat generic. While Scripture verses are included on each page, the activity can be used with a variety of Bible stories. This approach was taken to give the activities wide application and to make them extremely flexible for you.

Use these activities to help students find the connection between Bible characters, events, and topics and their everyday lives as children who are washed clean of sin daily. Adapt them to a specific lesson you are teaching and to the needs and abilities of your students. Make them your own!

Many of the activities suggested here can be completed by individual students but some may be readily adapted to small groups or even the whole class. As you consider how these projects can facilitate your teaching of Bible lessons, allow yourself time to brainstorm ideas and ways to make the most of them. And remember, the process is more valuable than the product. The hands-on opportunities you give your students will generate excitement for learning and joy for creativity as they learn God's Holy Word.

Bless you,

Jenifer Hosch

ACTIVITY 1

Bible Bookmark

Design two bookmarks about your Bible story. Use them to keep your place as you read the precious Word of God.

Blessed is the one who reads the words of this prophecy, and blessed are those who hear it and take to heart what is written in it. Revelation 1:3

Decorate both sides!

Blessed is the one who reads the words of this prophecy, and blessed are those who hear it and take to heart what is written in it.
Revelation 1:3

Book Cover

Imagine that you are an illustrator who has been asked to design the cover of a book about your Bible story. Remember that the cover of the book is the first thing someone sees. The picture and the lettering for the title should draw attention to the book and give the reader a hint about the story. Knowing this, design the book for someone who has never read the Bible.

But these are written that you may believe that Jesus is the Christ, the Son of God, and that by believing you may have life in His name. John 20:31

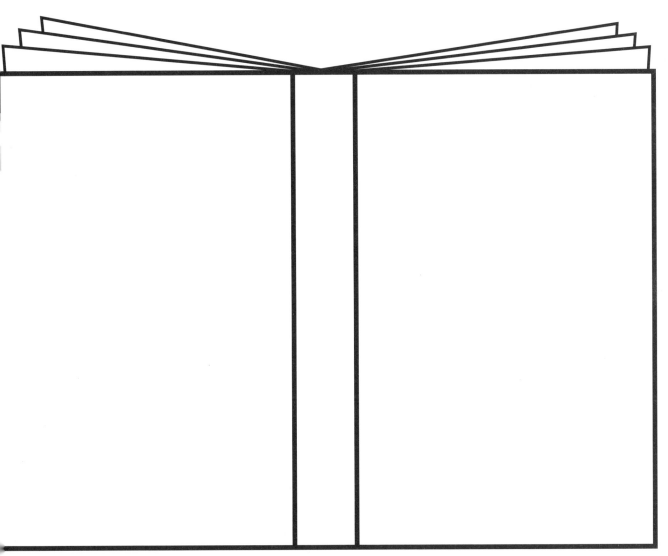

ACTIVITY 3

Portrait of a Hero

Draw a portrait of the main character in the Bible story you studied. Remember that Jesus Christ is the greatest hero of all.

Let your gentleness be evident to all. The Lord is near. Philippians 4:5

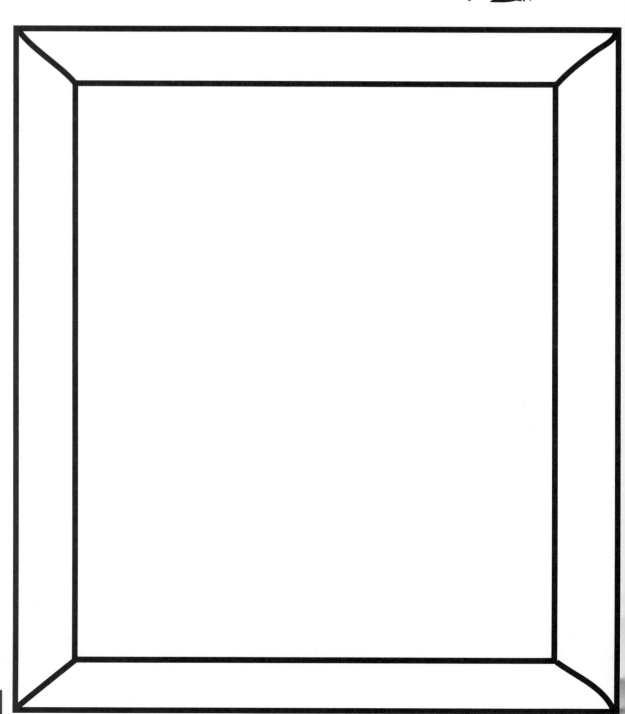

Crossword Puzzle

Choose at least 10 words from your Bible story. Make up clues for each word. Write the words on the grid, making sure to overlap words so they connect. Write the number for each clue at the beginning of the word it refers to. Color in the blank spaces.

Make the crossword puzzle by copying the numbers into the correct squares on the blank grid on the next page—but leave out the words. Color in the blank spaces. Then write the clues on the blanks at the bottom of the page. Give the puzzle to a friend to solve.

Fix these words of mine in your hearts and minds.
Deuteronomy 11:18

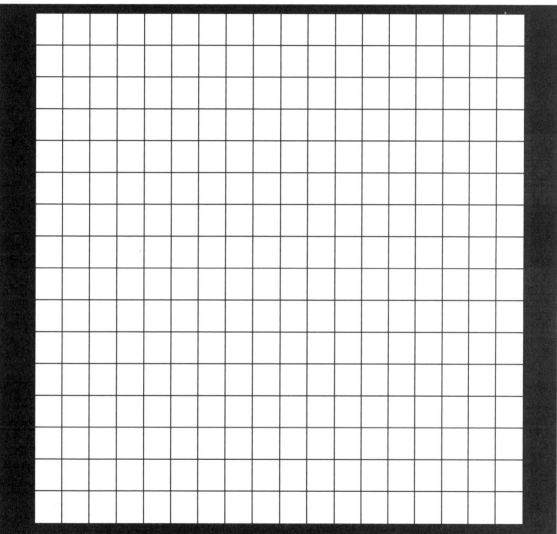

ACROSS:

_____

_____

_____

_____

DOWN:

_____

_____

_____

Crossword Puzzle

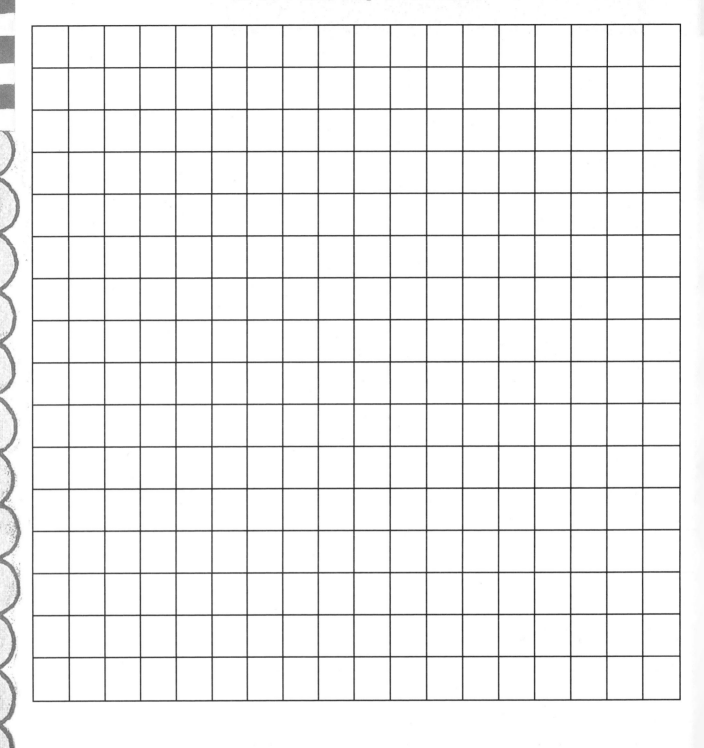

ACROSS:

_____
_____
_____
_____

DOWN:

_____
_____
_____
_____

Haiku

Haiku is a type of poetry that was first written in Japan more than 700 years ago. Haiku poems have 3 lines containing a total of 17 syllables. The first line has 5 syllables. The second line has 7 syllables. And the third line has 5 syllables. This is an example of haiku:

¹ ² ³ ⁴ ⁵
Samson was a man

¹ ² ³ ⁴ ⁵ ⁶ ⁷
Whose hair had never been cut.

¹ ² ³ ⁴ ⁵
Until Delilah!

Now it's your turn! Think about your Bible lesson. Praise God with a haiku about what you learned.

Line 1–5 syllables:

_____

Line 2–7 syllables:

_____

Line 3–5 syllables:

_____

All Scripture is God-breathed. 2 Timothy 3:16a

ACTIVITY 6

Cinquain

The word cinquain comes from the French word cinq, which means five. A cinquain is a poem with 5 lines. Here is a guide for writing a cinquain:

First line—one word giving the title
Second line—two words describing the title
Third line—three words expressing an action
Fourth line—four words expressing a feeling
Fifth line—another word for the title

Here are two examples of cinquains.

Ruth

Young woman
Leaving her home
To follow Naomi's God
Daughter-in-law

Peter

Fisherman disciple
Following, believing, preaching
Fiery, brash, repentant, strong
Rock!

Now it is your turn. Write a cinquain about someone or something in your Bible lesson.

_____

_____

_____

_____

_____

_____

Continue in what you have learned and have become convinced of, because you know those from whom you learned it. 2 Timothy 3:14

BIBLE LIMERICK

A limerick is a poem with five lines. The first, second, and fifth lines rhyme and the third and fourth lines rhyme. Here is an example of a limerick.

There once was a judge named Ehud
Who was asked to do what he could
To kill a fat man
In an enemy land.
He thought a double-edged sword would be good.

Write a limerick about the Bible story you've been reading.

Title: _____

_____

_____

_____

_____

_____

The unfolding of your words gives light; it gives understanding to the simple. Psalm 119:130

Design a Banner

Think about your Bible story and the victory we have in Jesus! Design a banner to illustrate the lesson it teaches. Make the banner from construction paper, felt, fabric, or other materials available to you. Hang your banner high in your classroom or at home. And give thanks to God that Jesus defeated sin, death, and the devil for us.

We will shout for joy when you are victorious and will lift up our banners in the name of our God. Psalm 20:5

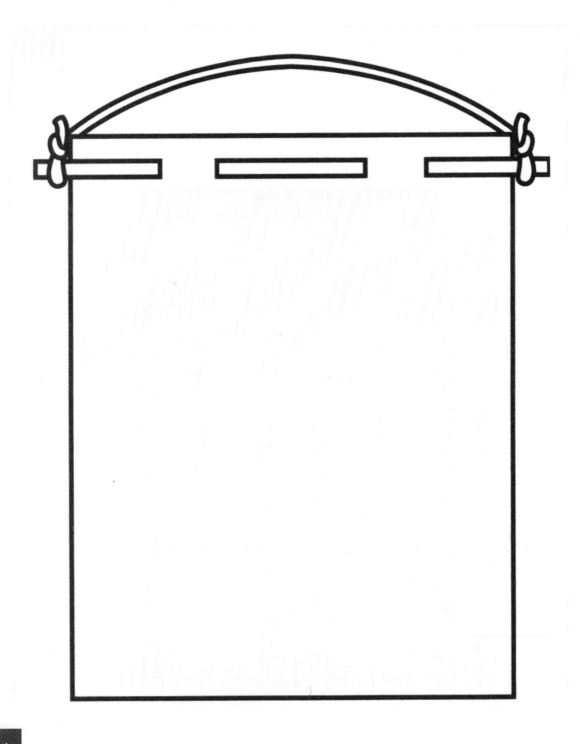

Filmstrip

Filmstrips are made of a series of pictures that show each scene in a story. In the film strips below, draw pictures that tell the Bible story you read. Some of the spaces could be filled with words, such as the title or the story, or "the end" in the last blank.

For everything that was written in the past was written to teach us, so that through endurance and the encouragement of the Scriptures we might have hope. Romans 15:4

15

ACTIVITY 10

Casting Director

In the first column, write the names of all of the characters in your Bible story. Now, imagine that you have been asked to cast actors to play the parts of these characters in a movie. Think of all the people you know—people in your class, in your family, and in your neighborhood. Who would you choose to play each part? Write the names of the actors you would choose on the lines in the second column across from the Bible story characters.

God, who has called you into fellowship with His Son Jesus Christ our Lord, is faithful. 1 Corinthians 1:9

BIBLE CHARACTERS

_____

_____

_____

_____

_____

_____

_____

_____

_____

_____

_____

ACTORS

_____

_____

_____

_____

_____

_____

_____

_____

_____

_____

_____

Word Search

Choose 20 words from your Bible lesson. Write them in the grid below. Write them vertically, horizontally, diagonally, forward, or backward in the spaces. After you have used all the words, fill in the rest of the squares with letters to hide the words you wrote. When your word search is complete, ask a friend to solve your puzzle.

It is the glory of God to conceal a matter; to search out a matter is the glory of kings. Proverbs 25:2

Find these words:

_____   _____   _____

_____   _____   _____

_____   _____   _____

_____   _____   _____

_____   _____   _____

_____   _____   _____

_____   _____

T-shirt

Draw a design on the T-shirt shape to illustrate the Bible story you studied. Try to keep the design on the center front of the shirt. Copy the design onto your own T-shirt. Then wear it to show others what you learned from God's Word!

"I will put My law in their minds and write it on their hearts." Jeremiah 31:33

Write a Song

The Bible is full of songs about God and what He does for us. Can you think of any? Write a song about the Bible story you studied today. A fun way to write a song is to use a melody you already know, such as "Jesus Loves Me," "To Your Temple, Lord, I Come," or "I Am Jesus' Little Lamb," and write new words. Then sing to the Lord a new song!

Speak to one another with psalms, hymns and spiritual songs. Sing and make music in your heart to the Lord. Ephesians 5:19

Paper Dolls

Think about the people in the Bible story you read. How do you imagine that they looked? Make a paper doll for each person in the Bible story. Use markers or crayons to color faces and clothing. Cut out the dolls. Then take them home to share the Bible story with your family.

So God created man in His own image. ... Male and female He created them. Genesis 1:27

Patterns may be used this size or enlarged to fit your needs.

Time Traveler

Imagine that you invented a machine to take you back to any period in time. You travel to the time of the Bible story you learned and you see the event as it is happening. Write about what you see.

I entered the time machine, and carefully pushed the button to secure the door closed. I set the time for my destination and pushed the lever to start the engine.

Suddenly...

_____

_____

_____

_____

_____

_____

_____

_____

_____

_____

_____

_____

_____

"I am the Alpha and the Omega," says the Lord God, **"who is, and who was, and who is to come, the Almighty." Revelation 1:8**

ACTIVITY
16

Travel Brochure

Travelers often look at brochures for information about places they will be visiting. Brochures show pictures and describe points of interest to encourage people to visit. Some brochures include maps or directions.

The places listed below are mentioned in Bible stories you may have read. Choose one of these Bible places. Design a travel brochure for this destination for a Bible times traveler. You may want to research the place in an encyclopedia or on the Internet before you get started.

Antioch

Jerusalem

Nazareth

Athens

Jordan River

Philippi

Dead Sea

Mount Carmel

Rome

Egypt

Mount of Olives

Sea of Galilee

Jericho

Mount Sinai

Ur

Other _____

_____

"Where you go I will go, and where you stay I will stay. Your people will be my people and your God my God." Ruth 1:16

Make a Map

People have been using maps for thousands of years. Maps show many things, such as the size and shape of a city or country, where buildings and landmarks are located, or roads and streets so people can know where to go. Make a map about the place you learned about in your Bible lesson. Show where important events in the story took place.

The earth is the LORD's, and everything in it. Psalm 24:1

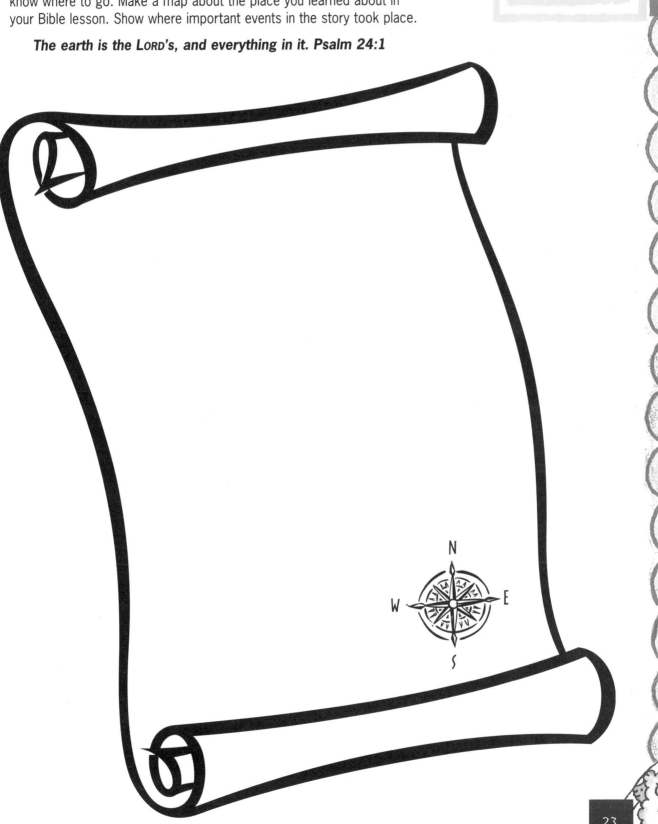

Letter

Many of Jesus' apostles wrote letters to tell people important things and to spread the Gospel. The Holy Spirit caused them to write about Jesus' teachings, about how to conduct business, and about what they had been experiencing. Sometimes in church these letters are called "epistles." We still read these letters in the Bible today. You hear parts of them when you go to a worship service at church.

The Bible story you read could be retold in a letter. Think about what the main character would write. Then write a letter on the scroll below.

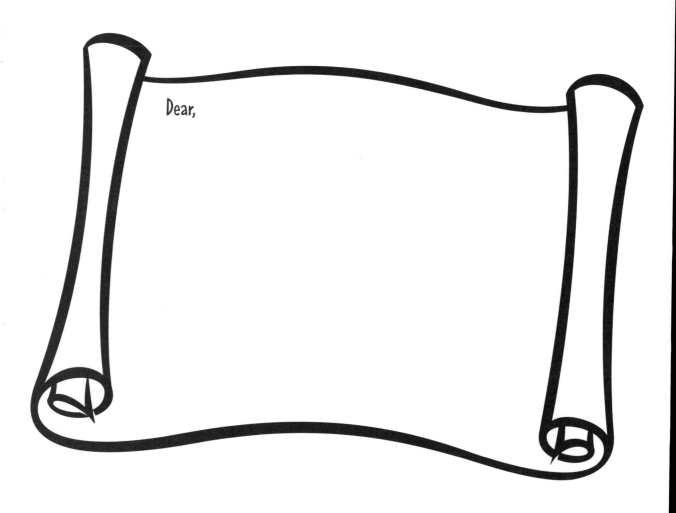

Dear,

After this letter has been read to you, see that it is also read in the church of the Laodiceans and that you in turn read the letter from Laodicea. Colossians 4:16

Bible Products

The Lord often uses things He created to bring to His people forgiveness and grace. He uses water in Baptism with His Word to give us faith and forgiveness and to make us members of His church. He uses bread and wine with His Word to give us His body and blood and forgiveness of sins. That's why we call this meal the "Lord's Supper."

Here is a list of people from the Bible. You will know some of the names very well. Other names may not be as familiar to you. Use a concordance to look up Bible stories about these characters. Then think of items that are associated with the person or the story. Write that item on the blank line a list of Bible products. Here are two examples: Noah's Animal Crackers and Cornelius's Used Armor.

Old Testament Characters

Adam's _____

Shem's _____

Abraham's _____

Rebekah's _____

Jacob's _____

Leah's _____

Aaron's _____

Joshua's _____

Ruth's _____

Gideon's _____

Samson's _____

Delilah's _____

Goliath's _____

David's _____

Solomon's _____

Jezebel's _____

Elijah's _____

Jehu's _____

Jeremiah's _____

Ezekiel's _____

Daniel's _____

Nehemiah's _____

Esther's _____

New Testament Characters

Joseph's _____

Herod's _____

Martha's _____

Lazarus's _____

Peter's _____

Matthew's _____

Salome's _____

Zacchaeus's _____

Mary Magdalene's _____

Nicodemus's _____

Pilate's _____

Paul's _____

Dorcas's _____

Lydia's _____

Silas's _____

Philip's _____

Timothy's _____

Luke's _____

James's _____

John's _____

Tertullus's _____

Caesar's _____

Is not the cup of thanksgiving for which we give thanks a participation in the blood of Christ? ...d is not the bread that we break a participation in the body of Christ? 1 Corinthians 10:16

ACTIVITY 20

Words and Shapes

Think about the main character in the Bible story you studied. Write this person's name in the shape of an object associated with the character. To get started, use a pencil to lightly draw a shape. To complete the activity, use a ballpoint or gel pen to write the name as many times as needed to complete the picture.

A good name is more desirable than great riches.
Proverbs 22:1a

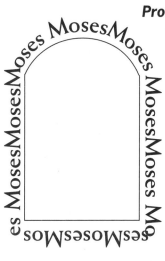

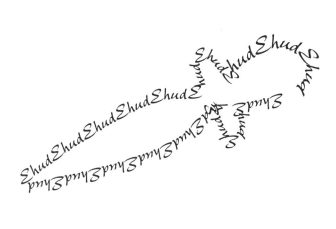

Bible ABCs

God inspired people to write His Holy Word into a book—the Bible. Books are written to tell others about important things. You can write your own ABC book that tells others about the Bible. Think of a word or person for each letter of the alphabet.

"I am the Alpha and the Omega, the First and the Last, the Beginning and the End." Revelation 22:13

A _____

B _____

C _____

D _____

E _____

F _____

G _____

H _____

I _____

J _____

K _____

L _____

M _____

N _____

O _____

P _____

Q _____

R _____

S _____

T _____

U _____

V _____

W _____

X _____

Y _____

Z _____

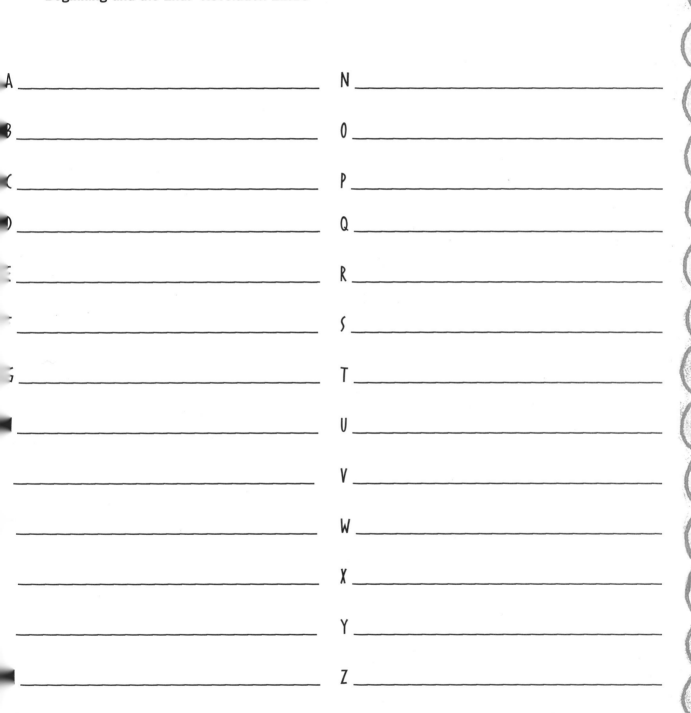

Candy Bingo

Teacher: Copy bingo cards for each student in your class. Make one copy of the grid below. Choose 24 words from the Bible lesson. Write questions for each of the 24 words onto the squares on the grid. Cut out the squares and place them in a small box or bowl.

List the 24 words on the blackboard or say the answers aloud so students can spell the words themselves. Have students write the 24 words in random order in the boxes on their bingo cards. Give each student 25 candy pieces. Pull a card from the bowl and ask the question. If students know the answer, they place a piece of candy on that square of their bingo card. The first to get 5 in a row wins. Play as many times as possible.

Student: Your teacher has given you a list of words that appear in the Bible story you read. Write the words in any box on your bingo card. When your teacher asks a question, find the answer on your bingo card and place a piece of candy on that box. Be sure to place a piece of candy on the free space. (Don't eat the candy until after the game is over!) The first person to get 5 answers in a row calls "bingo" and wins the game.

B I N G O

		FREE		

Remember the wonders He has done, His miracles, and the judgments He pronounced. 1 Chronicles 16:12

Autobiography

You have read a Bible story about a real person who lived a long time ago. Imagine that you are the person in the Bible story. Write your autobiography.

Title: _____

_____
_____
_____
_____
_____
_____
_____
_____
_____
_____
_____
_____
_____
_____
_____
_____
_____
_____
_____
_____
_____
_____

Consequently, you are no longer foreigners and aliens, but fellow citizens with God's people and members of God's household, built on the foundation of the apostles and prophets, with Christ Jesus Himself as the chief cornerstone. Ephesians 2:19–20

ACTIVITY 24

Family Tree

God makes us His children through water and Word when we are baptized. We are part of His family. In Baptism, we enjoy the fruits of the tree of life. The Bible tells us about other families and sometimes even gives us a family tree. For example, the first chapter of the book of Matthew tells us Jesus was a descendant of King David, who was a descendant of Abraham.

On the tree below, write the names of the people in your family. Start with yourself by writing your name on the trunk of the tree. Then write the names of your parents, and their parents, and so on.

Blessed are those who wash their robes, that they may have the right to the tree of life and may go through the gates into the city. Revelation 22:14

30

Newspaper Reporter

Make a newspaper about the Bible lesson you studied. Write several news articles about different aspects of the Bible story. The only way we know anything about God's salvation in Christ is because it was written down. The "Good News" is written in the words of the apostles and prophets.

To begin writing a news article, you must first begin with notes. Give short answers to these questions.

1. Who is the story about? _____

_____

2. Where did the story take place? _____

_____

3. When did it take place? _____

_____

4. What happened? _____

_____

5. Why is this story important? _____

_____

Now you have the information you need to write a rough draft of your story. On a separate piece of paper, write your story. Make changes to the story until you think it is finished. (Do this for each story you write.)

Now you are ready to complete your newspaper. Copy the stories in the columns on the newspaper page. Draw a picture about your lead story. Include headlines.

Jesus took the Twelve aside and told them, "We are going up to Jerusalem, and everything that is written by the prophets about the Son of Man will be fulfilled." Luke 18:31

THE BIBLE TIMES

Issue 1
FREE

Date

Samson's Riddles

Samson loved riddles. He told one at a wedding banquet (Judges 14:12–18). Write riddles about your Bible story.

Example: Which Bible character am I?

My name sounds like something good for lunch, but Moses would not eat it. I was on a long cruise, but it was not a vacation.

Answer: Ham

Answer:

Answer:

Answer:

Let the wise listen and add to their learning, and let the discerning get guidance—for understanding proverbs and parables, the sayings and riddles of the wise. Proverbs 1:5–6

Epitaph

The epitaph for the child of God is written in Romans 6. You died with Christ and you rose with Christ. Christ is your life. Some tombstones have a few words or a saying about the person buried there. This is called an epitaph. What would you write on the tombstone of the main character in your Bible story? Think about what was most important about that person and write the epitaph in the tombstone.

PETER
Fisher
of Men

If we have been united with Him like this in His death, we will certainly also be united with Him in His resurrection. Romans 6:5

Do You Want to Be a Millionaire?

In the popular television game show, "Who Wants to Be a Millionaire?" people compete for prize money by correctly answering questions. Use the Bible story you studied to create your own version of this game show. Write 15 questions about the story. Chose a contestant. Let the contestant have three "lifelines": class votes, ask a friend, 50/50. Then ask the questions you've written. If the contestant is not certain about an answer, he can use a lifeline to help.

$100 _____

A._____   B. _____

C._____   D. _____

$200 _____

A._____   B. _____

C._____   D. _____

$300 _____

A._____   B. _____

C._____   D. _____

$500 _____

A._____   B. _____

C._____   D. _____

In Him we have redemption through His blood, the forgiveness of sins, in accordance with the riches of God's grace. Ephesians 1:7

$1,000 _____

A._____   B. _____

C._____   D. _____

$2,000 _____

A._____   B. _____

C._____   D. _____

$4,000 _____

A._____   B. _____

C._____   D. _____

$8,000 _____

A._____   B. _____

C._____   D. _____

$16,000 _____

A._____   B. _____

C._____   D. _____

$32,000 _____

A._____   B. _____

C._____   D. _____

$64,000 _____

A._____   B. _____

C._____   D. _____

$125,000 _____

A._____   B. _____

C._____   D. _____

$250,000 _____

A._____   B. _____

C._____   D. _____

$500,000 _____

A._____   B. _____

C._____   D. _____

$1,000,000_____

A._____   B. _____

C._____   D. _____

ACTIVITY 29

Acrostic

An acrostic is a word puzzle in which the first letters of a group of words make a word or phrase. Make an acrostic about your Bible story from the phrase below, "Search the Scriptures." Look for words in the Bible story that start with each letter shown here.

S _____

E _____

A _____

R _____

C _____

H _____

T _____

H _____

E _____

S _____

C _____

R _____

I _____

P _____

T _____

U _____

R _____

E _____

S _____

Now the Bereans were of more noble character than the Thessalonians, for they received the message with great eagerness and examined the Scriptures every day to see if what Paul said was true. Acts 17:11

Stained Glass Window

For centuries, stained glass windows have been used in church buildings to illustrate Bible stories or themes. For example, Jesus as the Good Shepherd is often shown in stained glass windows. Use the shape below to design your own stained glass window to illustrate the Bible story you studied.

Let your light shine before men, that they may see your good deeds and praise your Father in heaven. Matthew 5:16

ACTIVITY 31

Bible Web Site

Web sites begin with an opening page and include links to other pages. Each page communicates information or a message. Design a Web site for the main character in your Bible lesson. Have at least 3 buttons or links to other pages on your Web site.

BIBLE HOME PAGE

Faith comes from hearing the message, and the message is heard through the word of Christ. Romans 10:17

Copy the square below to add additional pages to your Web site.

Buttons
Write words on the buttons below, then cut and glue to the Web pages.

Top 10 Reasons

People like to make lists. You may have seen lists of Top 10 Songs or Top 10 Books. Some people also list reasons. For example, there might be a list of the top 10 reasons for doing your homework. All the reasons for God's Word are always related to the work of Jesus Christ and what He does to save sinners. Review your Bible story. How does the message relate to what Jesus did for salvation? Write the top 10 reasons as to how this Bible story is related to Christ and what He has done for salvation. Include things Christ gives to you in church where He comes to serve you.

10. _____

9. _____

8. _____

7. _____

6. _____

5. _____

4. _____

3. _____

2. _____

AND

1. _____

And beginning with Moses and all the Prophets, He explained to them what was said in all the Scriptures concerning Himself. Luke 24:27

42

Make a Mobile

A mobile is a sculpture that hangs from the ceiling. It is made up of similar shapes or items. Each item is hung so the mobile is balanced and so it moves in the breeze or if it is touched. On the pattern below, design a mobile about the Bible story you read. Transfer the designs to construction paper or poster board. Color, cut, and hang the shapes to make your own mobile.

"The grass withers and the flowers fall, but the Word of our God stands forever." Isaiah 40:8

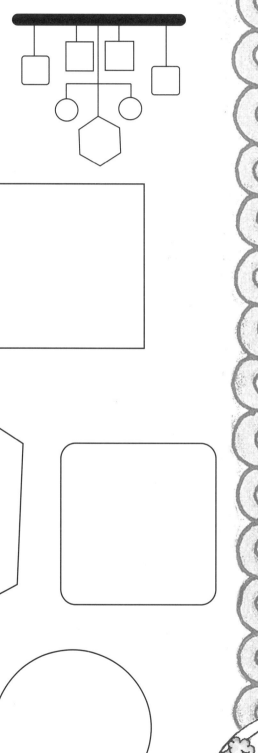

43

Board Game

Everyone enjoys board games. Use these pages to design a board game about your Bible story. Give your game a name. Design the playing pieces and the way the pieces will move on the board. Write the rules to the game. Then invite a friend to play the game with you. As you put your board game together, design it to include God's Law and Gospel. His Law is everything you must or must not do, like "love your neighbor." The Gospel is what God does for salvation and in your place and then gives it to you. In the Gospel, faith is given and so is the victory of life—heaven. It is already yours. In the Christian game of life, you already know that you win.

Title: _____

Game Pieces:

Copy and cut out the gamepieces. Draw an image or write a Bible verse on each side. Then fold on the dotted lines and tape the bottom of each piece.

Rules: _____

_____

_____

_____

_____

_____

_____

_____

_____

I press on toward the goal to win the prize for which God has called me heavenward in Christ Jesus. Philippians 3:14

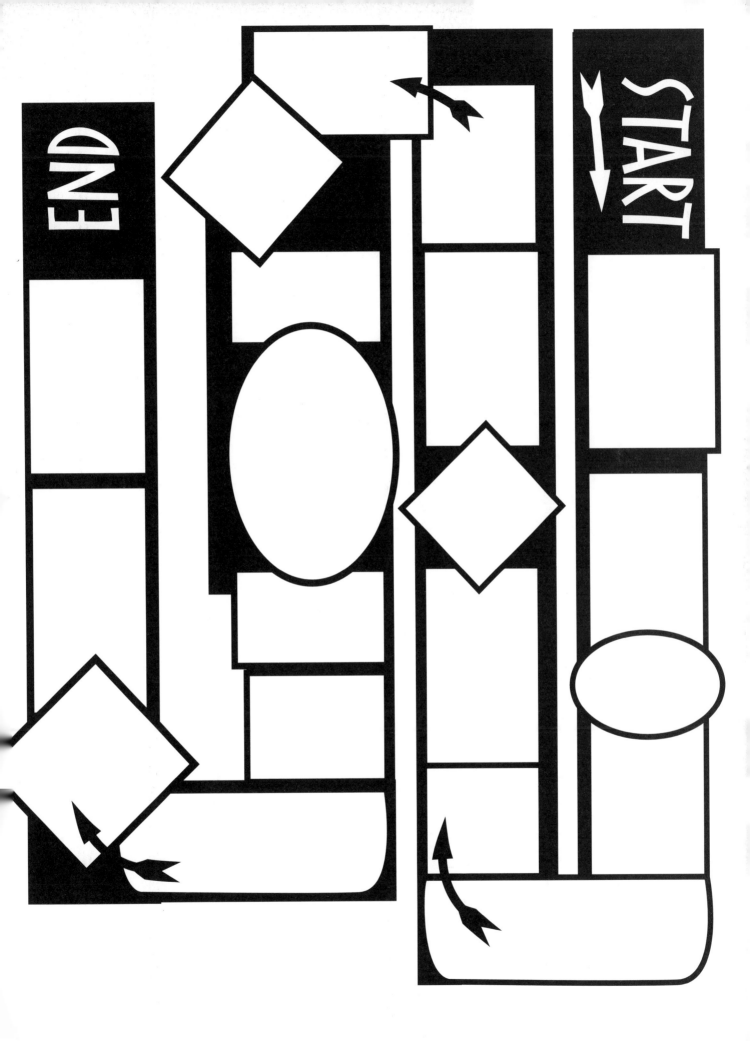

ACTIVITY 35

Time Line

The Bible is like a time line. It begins with the creation of the world and tells about events in history. At the same time, it tells us that God had no beginning and He has no end. Make a time line about your Bible lesson. First, think of five to ten important events in the story. Add events from Jesus' life, death, and resurrection.

1. _____
2. _____
3. _____
4. _____
5. _____
6. _____
7. _____
8. _____
9. _____
10. _____

Now place these events in chronological order on the time line.

Beginning

_____
_____
_____
_____
_____
_____
_____
_____
_____
_____

Ending

"The time has come," He said. "The kingdom of God is near. Repent and believe the good news!"
Mark 1:15

Museum Exhibit

Imagine that you have been asked to prepare a museum exhibit about the Bible character in the story you studied. What artifacts would you include? Would you include pictures, a statue, a life-size diorama? What information would you include for people to read? Design the exhibit here.

*I know, O L*ORD*, that a man's life is not his own; it is not for man to direct his steps. Jeremiah 10:23*

Bible Advertisement

Advertising is used to give information and to get attention. Ads usually include a "call to action," or a way for the person reading them to respond. This might be a phone number or a Web site address. Pretend that you are an advertiser who must create an ad for the Bible story you have read. Write a catchy slogan or headline, draw a logo or picture, and include a call to action.

"Go into all the world and preach the Good News to all creation." Mark 16:15

Read a Bible verse today!

"Go into all the world and preach the Good News to all creation." Mark 16:15

www.mark16:15.com

Draw your advertisement in the box below.

Point of View

"Point of view" is a term used in literature to describe the angle the story is told from. One character's point of view may differ from another. For example, if the shepherds and Joseph were to tell the Christmas story, their stories would be different because they would have different points of view.

Tell the Bible story you read from another point of view. Choose a character other than the main character and write what happened from that person's point of view. Remember that the cross of Christ and His victory over sin, death, and the devil is the real point of view from which every Christian understands all things.

View from the _____

_____

_____

_____

_____

_____

_____

_____

_____

_____

_____

_____

_____

_____

_____

_____

_____

_____

_____

_____

_____

_____

"Therefore everyone who hears these words of Mine and puts them into practice is like a wise man who built his house on the rock." Matthew 7:24

Party Time!

It's time to celebrate! Did you know that when you go to church and the Lord's Supper is offered, it is called the "celebration" of the Lord's Supper? Jesus calls those who are baptized and have learned His Word to enjoy the celebration of His resurrected body and blood in the bread and wine.

Plan a party for the main character in your Bible story. Think about what kind of party you would give, who would be invited, what you would serve, what party favors you would give, and what entertainment you would have. Then, design an invitation.

Type of party   _____

Guest list   _____

Refreshments   _____

Party favors   _____

Entertainment   _____

INVITATION COVER

You Are Invited

to a Celebration!

Invitation instructions: Copy the card on page 51. Cut out the square and fold on the dotted lines. Decorate the front cover and write party information inside.

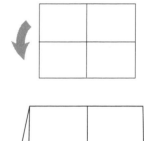
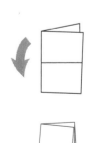

And Mary said: "My soul glorifies the Lord and my spirit rejoices in God my Savior." Luke 1:47

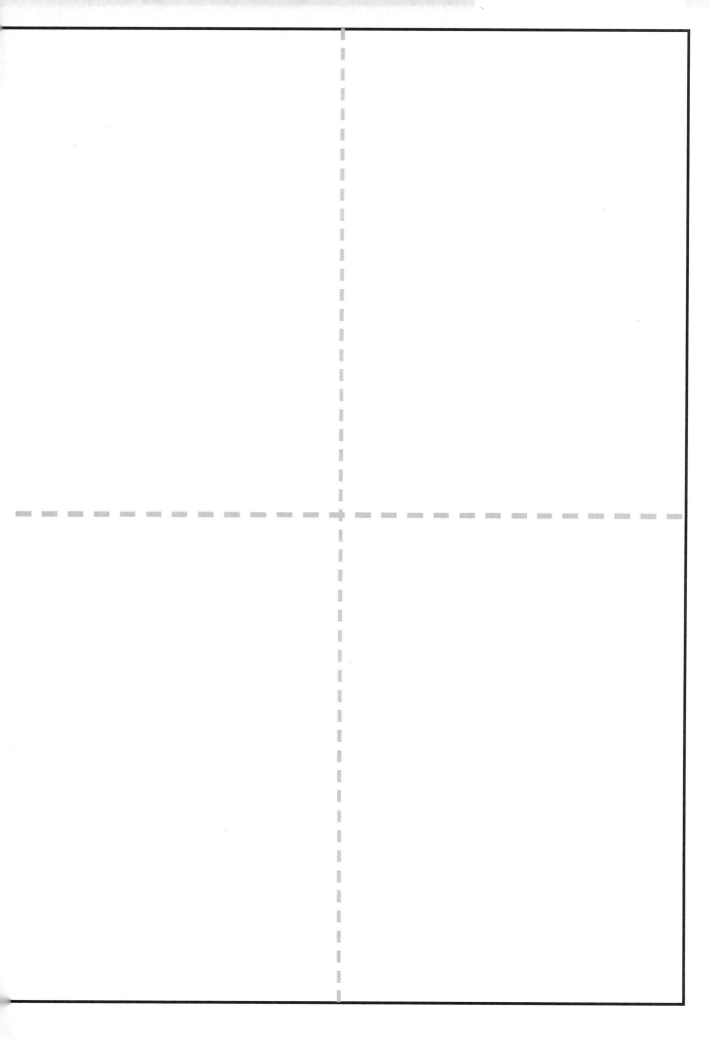

Pictures from Shapes

Color and cut out these shapes. Then have fun arranging them to make pictures. Think about the Bible story you read. How might you use these shapes to create a picture about the Bible story? When you have created a picture you are satisfied with, carefully glue the shapes in place on a piece of paper. Use a pencil or marker to write the Scripture reference (the Bible book, chapter, and verse) at the bottom of the page.

Show the wonder of Your great love, You who save by Your right hand. Psalm 17:7

Postage Stamp

Postage stamps are used on letters as a payment made so they will be delivered from one place to another. Many people collect stamps as a hobby. Postage stamps often have pictures of famous people or things. For example, presidents, actors, trees, cars, and even cartoon characters have been on stamps. Think about the people and things in the Bible lesson you studied. Design a postage stamp that shows someone or something from the story.

"By their fruit you will recognize them." Matthew 7:20

FREE

"By their fruit you will recognize them."
Matthew 7:20

53

Word Poster

Design a word poster about one of the people in the Bible story you read. Start by making a list of 10 or more words that describe this character. For example, for Jesus you might list Savior, King, Lord, Lamb, Shepherd, Messiah, and so on.

On your poster, make the most important words bigger and bolder than the other words. Arrange the words in an interesting pattern. You may add pictures or designs to your poster to make it more interesting.

Words:

_____ _____ _____

_____ _____ _____

_____ _____ _____

_____ _____ _____

[Mary said] "For the Mighty One has done great things for me—holy is His name. His mercy extends to those who fear Him, from generation to generation." Luke 1:49–50

King   SAVIOR   LAMB

Lord   SHEPHERD   MESSIAH

Make a Postcard

Have you ever gotten a postcard? Perhaps a friend or relative sent one to tell you about a vacation or to invite you to a party. Think about the main character in your Bible story. Make a postcard the character might write to a friend or relative. What would he or she say? From where would the postcard be sent?

Such confidence as this is ours through Christ before God. Not that we are competent in ourselves to claim anything for ourselves, but our competence comes from God. 2 Corinthians 3:4–5

Picture

Message

Place
Stamp
Here

ACTIVITY 44

Puppet Show

The Bible story you learned can be told by puppets. Draw your puppets in the space below. Puppets can be copied onto paper, colored and cut, then glued to craft sticks or plastic spoons. Write the script for your puppet show. Space is given for three scenes, but you can use as many scenes as you need to tell the story.

Setting: _____
_____
_____

Characters: _____
_____

Plot: _____
_____
_____

Scene 1: _____
_____
_____

Scene 2: _____
_____
_____

Scene 3: _____
_____
_____

For in the gospel a righteousness from God is revealed, a righteousness that is by faith.
Romans 1:17

Patterns may be used this size or enlarged to fit your needs.

ACTIVITY 45

Cross Stitch

Design a cross-stitch pattern for your memory verse. This can be done by writing key words or by drawing a symbol such as a cross or a heart. To create the pattern, fill in the squares on the grid below. Keep the design simple by using only a few colors.

How sweet are your words to my taste, sweeter than honey to my mouth! Psalm 119:103

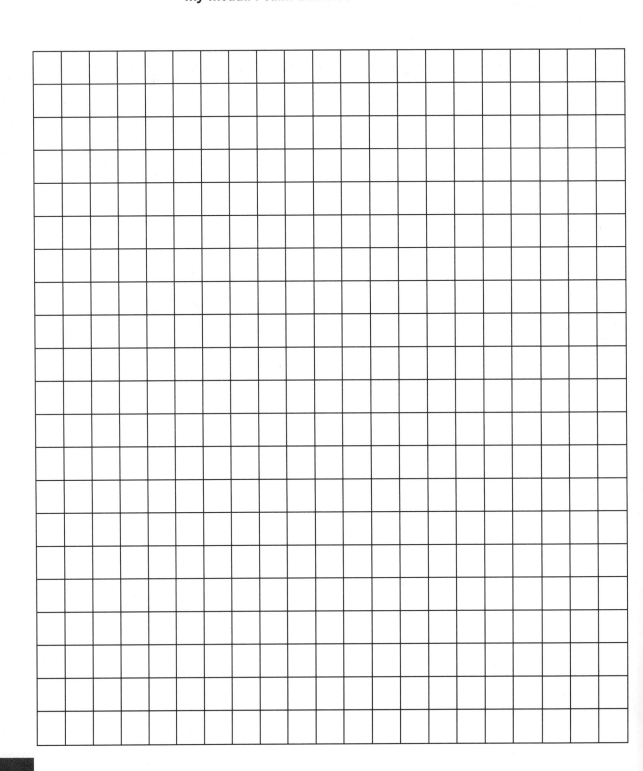

Bulletin Board

Plan a bulletin board about your Bible lesson. The title on the bulletin board should be short and catchy; it can be a verse or a part of a verse. The picture should tell something about the story and be eye catching. Decide what kind of border you will use. Color your design.

Tie [My words] as symbols on your hands and bind them on your foreheads. Write them on the doorframes of your houses and on your gates. Deuteronomy 6:8–9

PEACE ON
EARTH
GOOD WILL
TO MEN

Rebus

Sometimes symbols or pictures are used instead of letters or words. One of the places you may see pictures used for words is a sign on a building. A rebus is a puzzle that uses pictures for words. For example, the rebus below spells "Isaac loved Rebekah."

I-saac loved Re-be-kah.

Make a rebus for a character, object, or verse related to your Bible story.

"For who has known the mind of the Lord that He may instruct him?" But we have the mind of Christ. 1 Corinthians 2:16

Dear Diary

We always know that God works in our life because His Word promises it. His Word is alive in our lives because we are baptized children of God.

Pretend you are the main character in the Bible story you read. What might you think? What happened in your life that shows you are a child of God? What things are happening in your life right now? How does repentance and receiving forgiveness daily help you in your life every day? Write a diary entry for the character in your story.

Date:_____

Dear Diary,

_____
_____
_____
_____
_____
_____
_____
_____
_____
_____
_____
_____
_____
_____
_____
_____
_____
_____

And we know that in all things God works for the good of those who love Him, who have been called according to His purpose. Romans 8:28

ACTIVITY
49

Puzzle

Make a jigsaw puzzle about the Bible lesson you learned.

First draw the picture. Color it with crayons or markers. Cut out the puzzle along the outline and glue it to a piece of stiff paper or poster board. Then use a black felt-tip pen or marker to draw puzzle shapes on top of the picture.

Keep shapes simple but remember to make sure each shape interlocks with the one next to it. Cut out each shape along the puzzle lines. Give your puzzle to a friend and share the Bible lesson.

If you like, use the puzzle shapes on the next page. Photocopy the puzzle, glue it to the back of your picture, and cut along the puzzle lines.

When I came to you, brothers, I did not come with eloquence or superior wisdom as I proclaimed to you the testimony about God. 1 Corinthians 2:1

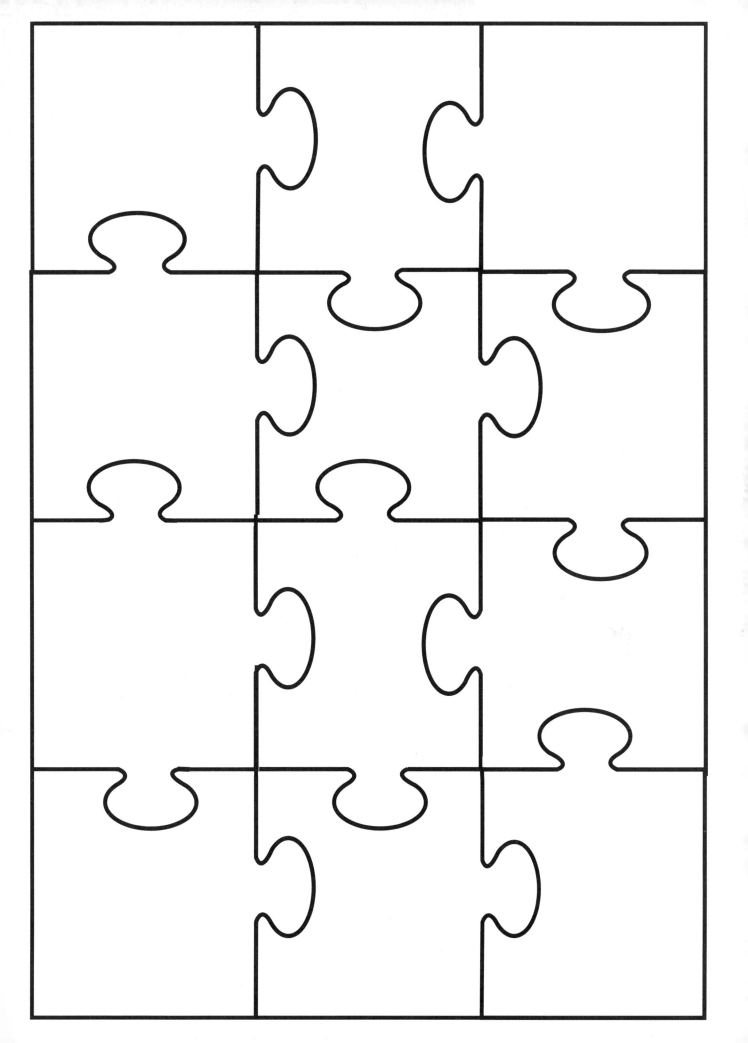

ACTIVITY 50

Building

Make a paper building to remind you of the places you go to learn about Jesus, worship, receive the Sacraments, and hear God's Word.

Copy the shape, draw a building, color it, and cut it out. You could make a church, a school, or your own home.

"Therefore everyone who hears these words of Mine and puts them into practice is like a wise man who built his house on the rock." Matthew 7:24

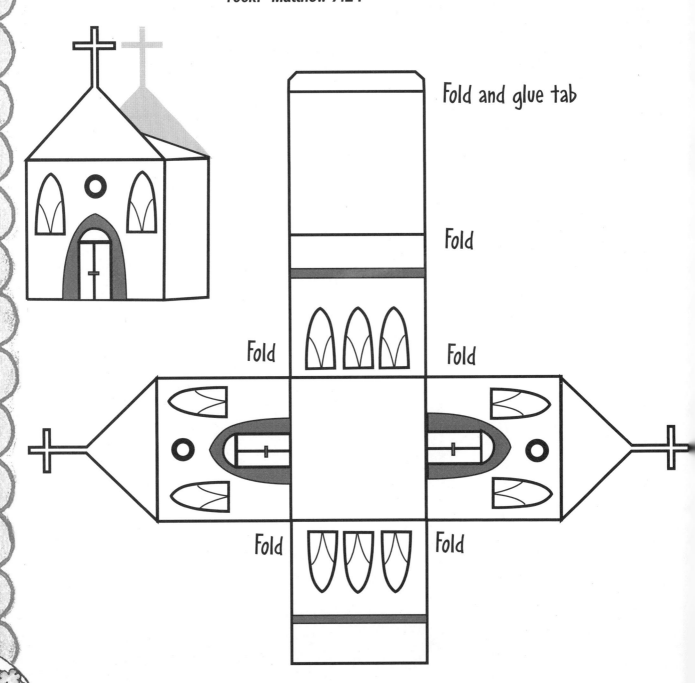

Fold and glue tab

Fold

Fold

Fold

Fold

Fold